My 1st lady
(Coming to terms)

I0836080

Santiego Rivers

My 1st lady

(Coming to terms)

Copyright © 2021 by Santiego Rivers

All rights reserved. This book may not be reproduced or transmitted in any form without the written permission of the author.

"no copyright infringement is intended."

ISBN 978-1-7376037-2-6

Men marry their mother, and women marry their father or lack thereof. **(In most cases)**

If a wife wants to know how her husband will treat her, she should examine his relationship with his mother.

His mother was the first woman in his life and should have laid the foundation on how to treat a woman.

Be aware of anyone who still suffers from mommy and daddy issues because you will become a victim of their unresolved trauma.

For many years, I had suffered from mommy issues that greatly affected my relationship with other women.

For a long time, I was in denial. I never thought that my relationship with my mother would play any part in how I treat women and the types of women that I choose.

I was wrong in both cases.

Time is the blessing that allows us to see that life and our understanding will change if we open our minds to the possibility.

This book will reveal the many lessons I was blessed to learn and how a boy became a man by shifting blame inwards instead of outwards to other people.

My growth as a man depended on me. Therefore, I needed to learn that despite the challenges and obstacles that I may have felt that other people put in my life, the decisions and choices I made were all on me.

If you decide to play the victim in life, you will always play the victim in life. But, if you choose to take control and responsibility for how you react to the things you will face in your life, you will be one step closer to obtaining inner peace. You are the only hero that you will ever need to save you.

I choose peace over war, and hopefully, this book will inspire you to do the same.

The beginning that I remember always start with my brother and my mother surrounded by her family.

I knew more about my fathers' parents and siblings than I knew about him. But, as a child, I did not know why that was the case?

Was it because of me? Did he not want to be around me? These are all the questions that go through the mind of a child. I am sure that my mother told me about my father, but unfortunately, I do not remember.

When one parent is missing from a child's life, the parent who is left raising that child not only plays the mother and the father, they also play the hero and the villain.

My mother played all the major parts in my life, for better or for worse. The older that I got, I viewed her more in the villain role, like how my kids viewed me at that age.

Why did I not view my father in that same light as a child? Well, the answer is simple. You must be present more often to be cast in the movie.

I will not say that my father was not around or that I did not have the opportunity to stay with him as a child. However, I will say that my father and the relationship he has with his kids deserve its own book, like what I wrote for my kids.

I have no issues with my father. However, time has allowed me the opportunity to learn; holding onto grudges, hate, and pain hurts you more than it affects others.

It took me many years to learn this lesson, but I am grateful that I could **learn, accept** and **apply** it to my life.

I want the same thing for my children because they also share my ability to hate and hold grudges that, unfortunately, I inherited from both of my parents.

My mother was the **1st**. She was the first person that I **loved** and became the first person that I grew to **hate**.

This statement is not something that I am proud of; it is the realization that I had to face before I learn to let go of my **hate** and **anger** to find **peace** in my life.

Since this book is about my relationship with my mother based on *my perspective*, I must be completely transparent.

This book is not to shed a bad light on my mother because I would only succeed in showing you my faults as a man.

This book explains the growth that I had to endure to become a better version of myself.

I love my mom. I can honestly say this because we had gone full circle repeatedly before being brave enough to realize that I can control how I react to what happens to me.

For me, to truly love someone, you must feel the same way when you think that you hate them.

Most people will not understand this, but ask someone who has been married a few decades to explain this to you.

Or ask someone who will beat you down for putting hands on their family member even though they don't like them all the time.

I love my mom, but I do not always like or understand the things that she does. I am sure that she feels the same way that I do regarding me.

Allow me to get back on topic

From a child's perspective, our parents are supposed to be perfect! However, there is no perfect parent, and there is no ideal child despite how we may feel personally about this statement.

When it comes to our parents being super parents:

- Who kisses or bruises when we get hurt?
- Who is tall enough to get the cookies off the top shelf when we can't reach them?
- Who helps us with our homework when it gets tough?
- Who checks the closet and under the bed when we think that we are in danger?

Our parents are the **superman** and the **superwoman** that we are lucky to have in our life.

My mom was and still is both people in my life.

What happens when we discover that our super moms and dads are not perfect? How does this shake the foundation of that child?

How can the person who built you up in life be the same person that makes you feel inferior?

The answer to this question is simple. People are human! We build people up, only to tear them down when they do not live up to every qualification we want them to fulfill.

It was not until I became a parent did I realize how hard it is to be a parent. I can't even imagine being a single mother and raising boys without their fathers' help.

As a child, we must find someone to blame for everything that goes wrong in our lives while taking credit for everything that goes right.

Why do we blame the person present in our life for our every failure but not our success? Because we are self-serving creatures. It will take growth and maturity to understand that people can teach us valuable lessons from their mistakes.

We pay closer attention to the mistakes that a person makes than the many good deeds that the person does by simply being present in our life.

My mom has always been present in my life, for better or for worse. My dad has been there when I needed him also.

My mom has many strengths that I love in a woman that I *unconsciously* seek in other women that I choose to have a serious relationship with.

The strengths/ qualities that my mom has that is a must for the woman in my life

My mom is what the old people call a **'Jack of all trades"**. She is skillful in the kitchen, yard, workforce, and every situation that she is needed.

My mom is not afraid of getting her hands dirty and clean them off to be a mother and a wife.

My mom never tried to party or hang out in the streets with my brother and me. She is not on social media half-naked or causing drama.

My mom dressed respectfully in public and knew how to behave in a manner that showed class.

My mom is what I consider a lady, but I know that she had her past like all of us. As a child, I was never embarrassed by my mother.

I work with young scholars for a living, and I have seen parents come to school, looking, smelling, and acting like street trash.

Alley Cat

No disrespect if you like that type of thing in your woman. I am not a fan of alley cats, even when I was an alley dog myself.

I have higher standards

Unconsciously, I have always been attracted to ***strong independent women of color***. The only thing that a weak and needy woman can do for me is point me in the direction of her strong independent friend.

Being with a solid independent woman is very tough. You can't be a weak individual because you will be eaten alive.

I will pass on a passive woman by nature, but I love a strong woman who is willing to be submissive to her alpha male.

My mom and I bumped heads so often because we were so similar in our mindset. I do not have half the skills that she possesses, but I have the boss mentality.

I said that we had a similar mindset because I learned that I needed to learn a different way that worked for me and my anger issues.

I saw how having a stubborn mindset was working out for my mom and dad from my perspective, and I did not want to have that for me.

I did not want to carry the same unresolved baggage that they both carry around today, from my perspective.

I saw how it affected my life and my relationship with people, and I was not fond of it.

I learned that people would not think and do as I do, and I can't think and do like other people. So, we must learn to respect and accept each person's differences.

Why try to win every argument if it divides you or hurts the people you love? Growing up around dominant/ headstrong people, one of two things will happen.

You will either become a **dominant/headstrong individual** or a **passive person**.

I am a gentle soul by nature, but I will not poke the bear within me and think it will not attack if I were you.

I have learned many lessons by watching my parents and making many of my own mistakes.

I criticized my parents for the same mistakes/ faults that I must deal with today within me.

As a child, you don't realize how young your parents were when they had you and the struggles of being a parent, especially a *single parent*.

I take back most of all the things I said and did to criticize my parents. However, the one thing that I learned that a parent could tell their child is that they were once the current age that they are now, and they understand how we think and act from an untrained mind in our youth.

Hopefully, we are blessed to be their age one day and compare an adult's thoughts and feelings to that of a child with them.

Time will change your perspective on many things.

Things time has allowed me the opportunity to see

I didn't know anything! Just because you feel a certain way does not make your feelings facts!

A child's perspective is not the reality of an adult, and the child will never understand the responsibility of being an adult.

As a parent/ adult, we must do what is needed and not always what is wanted. There will be many mistakes along the way because being a parent does not come with a handbook or a reset button. Parenting is not a game!

When you have kids at an early age, life will be tough!

Life is not like the *Brady Bunch* or the *Cosby* show. We must create the happy ending that we want in our life.

Even if you are a young adolescent or 13 going on 30, life is more than you can imagine.

Yes, you may have experienced trauma and grief in your childhood that you should not have faced.

You survived it physically, so for your sanity, you must learn to survive it mentally. So, forgive, but you don't have to forget.

Let it go! Do this for you and your well-being. Don't worry about doing it for someone else. They have probably forgotten about the incidents that you are still reliving each day of your life.

Stop holding someone to their past and the things that they did to you. Are those people still the same person today as they were in the past, or are you still stuck in the past mentally?

Seek God first, then **counseling.** If you can't move forward with your life, you will forever be stuck in your past.

If you are reading this book and getting into your feelings, you have not moved on. We should find a way to free our minds so that we can lighten up our load.

Give your trouble and burdens to God and find peace in your life.

I carried all my hatred and pain as far as I was going to take them. I refuse to take them any further on my journey.

What I had to do was learn to focus on the things that I could control. Luckily, the one thing that I can control is how I responded to the situations that my mother and I went through.

First and foremost, I came to accept that I will always love and respect my mother. So why would I ever decide to go to war with her?

If there is no enemy within, the enemy on the outside can do no harm. Therefore, my mother is not my enemy.

We may not always agree on everything, but I still know my place as a child of my mother.

When I feel that my emotions will get the best of me, I have learned to take a step back and meditate because I know that my prayers will be answered.

Learning how to **treat, respect**, and **love** the first lady in your life, will make it easier to do the same thing for the last lady that you will have in your life if you are willing to put in the needed work.

I didn't say **lucky** because **luck** is when **preparation** meets **opportunity.** You must be willing to put in that work.

Are you working on the things that will help you become a better person or sitting around mad?

If you are sitting there reading this book with your face frowned up, taking notes of everything you don't like about this book, you are not working on becoming the best version of yourself.

You can lie to other people, but you cannot lie to yourself.

I had to look in the mirror more than once and get to the point where I had to address the main culprit in the room. **(Myself)**

Who will you discover when you take an honest look at yourself in the mirror and stop blaming your parents for the baggage you still carry today?

Loving the first lady in my life has helped me to change my life for the better.

www.ingramcontent.com/pod-product-compliance
Lightning Source LLC
LaVergne TN
LVHW050612100826
845148LV00015B/3235
* 9 7 8 1 7 3 7 6 0 3 7 2 6 *